GW01375172

super try again

Also by Roddy Lumsden

Yeah Yeah Yeah
The Book of Love
Roddy Lumsden is Dead
The Bubble Bride
Mischief Night: New and Selected Poems

The Message: crossing the tracks between poetry and pop
(edited with Stephen Troussé)

Anvil New Poets 3 (edited with Hamish Ironside)

Vitamin Q: a temple of trivia lists and curious words

super try again
roddy lumsden

Donut Press

Published by Donut Press in February 2007.

Donut Press, PO Box 45093,
London, N4 1UZ.
www.donutpress.co.uk

Printed and bound by
Aldgate Press,
3 Gunthorpe Street, London, E1 7RQ.

Thanks to Vicky and Elizabeth for
their artwork assistance.

ISBN-10: 0955360404
ISBN-13: 9789550360404

Copyright © Roddy Lumsden, 2007.
All Rights Reserved.

The right of Roddy Lumsden to be identified
as author of this work has been asserted
by her in accordance with the Copyright,
Designs and Patents Act 1988.

A CIP record for this book is available
from the British Library.

Foreword

The poems here all take as their starting point existing texts such as a paragraph of prose, a song lyric, a piece of graffiti. One or two are based on spoken words – a conversation or a dream phrase. Notes at the back explain the source for each poem. It struck me that, just as you can translate between languages, you ought to be able to translate between genres of writing.

Some of the pieces were written using particular methods of composition. In what I've termed an *overlay*, the writer takes a piece of (usually) non-poetry and turns it into a poem, keeping some aspects of the original (the length, say, or the narrative structure or some of the language). It's a sort of mapping process, and more than just using something as inspiration. The idea is that the other text is like a bare table over which you drape the fabric of a poem. Meanwhile, in a *homeopathic poem*, you rewrite and rewrite a piece of text, or even someone else's poem, until it feels like your own.

RcL

Acknowledgements

Acknowledgements are due to the editors of the following
publications and websites in which some of these poems
first appeared: *Magma*, *Poetry* (Chicago), *Automatic Lighthouse* (Tall
Lighthouse, 2006), *Limelight* (*www.thepoem.co.uk*), the Poetry Society
website (*www.poetrysociety.org.uk*) and *Showcase* (*www.laurahird.com*).

'Coster Colony' was commissioned by Blue Nose Poets /
Museum of London for the 'Lost London' project.

Thanks are due to Nina Blackett and Ahren Warner for their
helpful advice on some of these poems.

Joanna Newsom's 'Peach, Plum, Pear' is included on the album
The Milk-Eyed Mender (Drag City, 2004).

Contents

A Story of Spice, 1
Cute, 2
Tyrol, 4
Tied-Up House, 6
Against Complaint, 7
Jackpot, 8
Shoreline Charismatic, 10
Salt, 11
Hunter's Stew, 12
Keepsakes, 14
The Boon of the Wind, 15
At the Heroes of Folklore Meet-up, 16
Cavian, 17
Poem Beginning With a Line By Roddy Lumsden, 19
Coster Colony, 20
To the Sea, 22

Notes, 24

This is unlike the story it was written to be
I was riding its back when it used to ride me
And we were galloping manic to the mouth of the source
We were swallowing panic in the face of its force

Joanna Newsom, 'Peach, Plum, Pear'

A Story of Spice

Since we are human and we seek
what is beyond the ear, behind
the yard's back wall, all that lies

outside our giddy orbis, we have sent
caravels and coracles and caravans
across tasky seas of sand or salt,

slow-blooming enterprise, our coins
thrown into such wells, our wishes
bright against a sullen sky

and have surrendered one in five
(a thumb lopped off) to pools of fire,
to brawling clans who came our way

as we went theirs, and all to bring
the scorch and tang in sacks and jars
with which our cooks will bind and brim

the evening air, while men draw ale
and women dance and children run
through golden fields to golden homes.

Cute

Before the sky shook loose that night
and the snow came, this terrible word

had passed my lips two times; first
when we saw a snail nosing along the lip

of the car-park. *Cute!* I clipped it
with my Chinese leather slip-on

then tapped again, the way a brother
would snap the obedient silence

in the monastery refectory by cracking
the top of a goose egg. *Don't*, you said,

not knowing this is how slugs are made,
set free from their jails. And later,

seeing the words *Shadow Boxer*
felt-tipped on the Gentlemen's wall,

I surrendered again that mellifluous bullet
of a word to the world. *Cute!* I thought,

a shadow boxer and a giant of graffiti
to boot, and showed the empty loo

my thumbs up, considering him, inky,
a quiet champion on a stained duvet,

punching towards the ceiling,
throwing shapes onto the mustard wall,

punching up at the snowy roof,
his mother snoring in the next room.

Tyrol

...where the moon sends shadows of pines
all across the rockface and giant saints
cascade on gable walls: Christopher
toting the infant; Florian dousing
the blazing house; the blood of the Cross
drooling from rooftop to wayside.

Though the paint now speckles and cracks
and the painters are sprung to dust,
I was there when those muralists swayed,
daring on their ladders, blessing
home after home, each face more pious,
each sword sharper in the Lord's resolve.

On the brow of the crag's brow, the convent
seems a swallow's nest, and in the tower
the newest sisters toll the bell; their gazes
fall far, upon a surging coach below
whose post-boy touts his horn and brags
a long note which rises in the dimming light,

rises till it fills a tear flashing in the eye
of the youngest nun, who grips the rope
and yanks it down, against herself,
until the speeding horses are distant specks
and the last faint echoes of the horn
are drowned beneath that brazen bell.

Tied-Up House

I snitch a pebble from the pier-side:
teeny, spray-soaked, worn to a bearing.
The gowling bay spins in a copper blur,
a thumb-size shrimp boat sways to shore.

I will not return now to the tied-up house
with its triple locks and welded snecks
and its citizens who yowl in the mirk
or stiffen in the soundless, month-long days,

where the ocean's roar loups from room
to room, salt-staining the unpainted walls.
I don't know where I got these bloody hands
or why a faint sobbing fouls the wind.

Against Complaint

Though the amaryllis sags and spills,
so do those my wishes serve, all along the town.
And yes, the new moon, kinked there in night's patch,
tugs me so – yet I can't reach to right the slant.
And though our cat pads past without a tail, some
with slinking tails peer one-eyed at the dawn, some
with eyes are clawless, some with sparking claws
contain no voice with which to sing
of foxes gassing in the lane.

                Round-shouldered pals
parade smart shirts, while my broad back supports
a scrubby jumper, fawn or taupe.

                The balding English
air their stubble, while some headless hero sports
a feathered hat. I know a man whose thoroughbred
grazes in his porch for want of livery.
There are scholars of Kant who can't find Kent
on the map, and men of Kent who cannot
fathom Kant.

        We who would polish off a feast have lain
late in our beds, our bellies groaning, throats on fire.
We who'd drain a vat of wine have drunk
our own blood for its sting.

                Each of us in tatters flaunts
one treasured garment flapping in the wind.

Jackpot

The season's triumphs: still
        and brackish water gleaming,
the log-stack at the wood's core,

        a rusky pony blissing
in the early dusk, as hammerflush
        dances from the anvil;

the owl moans through late sun haze
        and the barnyard reels
with shadowy dens for hiding.

        Glimpsed at a window,
past sifting peat smoke, a brisk girl
        near calm, known to us all.

That the depths beneath the bridge
        are cold and cruel
is not in question, though no one yet

        will venture a name for
this stout boy striding out
        whose fate it is to plunge

into the mile-deep pool
           and rope the great bell, lost to us
these thousand years.

Shoreline Charismatic

I have seen the sea-edge
        ambassador to stars
                gathering and greeting

and the track to the sea
        zedding north through gorse
                compass-constant

but since each night
        I am fetched into
                the grasp of sleep

I have never seen
        the blackthorn draw forth
                needles from the branch

that they might stitch
        each salted drop
               – the sea itself –

a miracle blink of
        viscous metal, lulling gases
                liquid grace

Salt

Since I will never decipher
        such crystalline wit
I dash it into a pool of stock

Beneath my bare foot
        the spilled grains grate
and I am full of such undimming luck

Its calibre threads my blood
        and when I cry I cry
a code you will not crack

A relic of advantage
        which drifts in sweat
or taints each compound lick

If you step out of your grifting sea
        I will hold you then
I will taste it on your cheek

Hunter's Stew

In every pan and kettle, stew gurgles
and pundits and poets circle
with half-boiled testaments, blind stabs
to nail its marvel smell, its omen stain,
its dab hand tricking on the lips.

But mere persuasions, diagnoses,
molly words can't catch its essence.
Not for the mouths of pale city wretches,
only those with lust in the singing voice
can *taste* it, those who know the shades

in the byways, who've cantered homeward,
sore, with the catch on their shoulders.
This is no weekday bubble-up, and not
your canteen casserole, this hunter's stew
squares up to you and grants you wishes.

New-lugged from the earth, cabbage
is the heart of the alchemy, sluiced and sliced,
tart and zesty, snaking in the pot,
welcoming with wanton arms choice collops
and cantles of gammon and game.

As scullions and skivvies gather and gaze,
flushed to the cheeks, mopping their temples,
the mishmash seethes, the geyser threatens
to blow, froth leaping at the pot's lip
lacing the air and flavouring the hour.

Be ready. Buff your arsenal of spoons,
give up your chases, charge your bowls
with the spoils of the cosmos. Ah, be brave.
Push through the hot fog to the stove
and make the copper kettles clang

and hide the stuff; let's see you yell
and yank it down – watch it disappear
like spring ice, like camphor, banished
to the dark within you, to the gullet's gloom,
the Stygian belly, the tarry, singing gut.

And peer through the steam, to see the pots
now scraped and scuppered, the cooks
glutted and dozing, with ladles in hand,
like minor fire gods, guarding the core
of a smoking and sacred volcano.

Keepsakes

Having failed for a third time to witness
the sight of sights – the sun
rising over the city of sand –

I took off due west from Tierra del Fuego
in an unmarked plane
and flew until I found dry land

which meant Tierra del Fuego, and lay
in a wind-tossed dune
where I could never grow tanned

and no one could see your name tattooed
in ink the colour of skin
or the lock of hair snuck in my hand.

The Boon of the Wind

A fool should never marry, unless a fool
come whispering by
        and they must found a village
– and never a city
        for cities are primed by the wise –
where they will tread paths and trim elms,
sow lawns and set ponds and fill their sacks
        with common treasure.

And if the wind should roll around the house
and find one spark
        to fan, of slender knowledge
– while fools lie
        stunned in one another's arms –
a boon might rouse the cinders
and ride the grate and a child will rise
        singing through smoke.

At the Heroes of Folklore Meet-up

Jack on the edge of the well was stripping a stout ash wand;
Jack, watching Jack and Jack swap third riddle tactics,
was under a spell and could not speak for a year and a day.

Jack carried a sack which grew heavier with each step
past Jack who gave his last morsels to a bearded stranger
and took his place round the campfire, between Jack and Jack.

Jack eyed the cursed bridge – beyond it, Jack, Jack and Jack
were wrestling in a meadow for the maiden's hand.
I bet you can't fill up this bowl with lies, said Jack

to Jack, who carried a beaming goose beneath one arm.
I strode in and rattled three times on the town hall door:
I've travelled quite some way, I said. *My name is Jack.*

Cavian

While riffing on my hipster policy,
a corvine brunette dabbled with her mane,
muttering beneath her jasmine breath
Luke Chapter 17 Verse 25.

A corvine brunette dabbled with her mane
as night got born. I knelt and testified
Luke Chapter 17 Verse 25.
A bloated, bad moon gadded up above.

As night got born, I knelt and testified.
The party snacks were laced with mescalin.
A bloated, bad moon gadded up above
the pyramid of Quatzaculcapetl.

The party snacks were laced with mescalin.
My left hand was a glass, my right a gun.
The pyramid of Quatzaculcapetl
was painted on a triptych in my brain.

My left hand was a glass, my right a gun.
The sainted widow, half flesh half metal,
was painted on a triptych in my brain
and dreaming of the convent on the meadow.

The sainted widow, half flesh half metal,
muttering beneath her jasmine breath
and dreaming of the convent on the meadow
while riffing on my hipster policy.

Poem Beginning With a Line By Roddy Lumsden

Each thinks the other blind:
his mouth was mobile and he had crooked teeth;
slowly – in a tight dress, cheating at truth –
her voice has gone the way of her orchestra.
Night covers the pond with its wing.

How does it tilt, then? In the direction of the ending:
as dusk came poor across the river, shimmering
under feint of stars in the dazzling rays,
making so much of this life seem invisible
and recorded as the memoirs of sad kings.

Coster Colony
(Drury Lane c1850)

'The Goose', young Harry and 'The King' –
the crossing-sweepers – steer me in
to a sharp-lit street, a courtyard split
by a cart-track – a stone-paved strip
the width of a costermonger's cart.
And in the narrow entry, women sit
with legs tucked up beneath their skirts,
taking on the shape of wine flasks,
as lifeless as caryatids
for this low temple and never seeming
to move, save for some times hissing
their wares: spliced onions, hands of herring.

Neighbours, a yard or two apart
lean from narrow attic windows
fat arms on the sill like cat's paws,
newsing on the day's thin takings,
the highwaymen and latest hangings.
Below, the barrow boys, pipe-smoking
in corduroy and brass buttons,
block the pavement outside the beershop.
Black brooms hang outside the sweep's shop
and peach-faced children perch on kerbstones;
women knitting, stitching linen,
brown men, dealing cards the colour

and quality of butcher's paper,
eye me up and down, intruder
into the hawker's home. The parlour
windows of the homes are shuttered
with old flap-tables. The coster's trucks,
all muddied from the morning's work,
are slaked down and stacked with stock:
waxy spuds and pennyworths
of pike-stiff fishes, meerschaum brown.
One might tell what each coster sells
by his refuse pile: a deep blue mound
of mussel shells, the mushy hulls

of cabbage, yellowing to broth;
punnets and pottles, cracked and stained
with berry-blood, broken sieves
scrawled with their owner's mark in red,
as sheep are. Above our heads,
the washing drips on drying poles:
grey petticoats which whip and lift
like flags hung out for the parade,
patched-up blankets with more holes
than one finds in a pigeon loft.
And ranging through the clots of cloud,
the noonday sun winks on and off.

To the Sea

Though the rill is lost in the topsoil,
sunk through stones, you will still find
the sea: listen for the fine bell
of a rain-drip as it lands
and don't presume the brook
as you chase it down the gorge
across the silvered rocks,
to pace the stream at the meadow's edge
which rolls and fills out till a torrent
rises and small fleets chance to ride
the river's flank from sweet to salt
below the brink where men have knelt
to pour their treasures into currents
unmeasured, to pay tribute to the tide.

Notes

A Story of Spice is an overlay of the opening paragraph of *Dangerous Tastes: The Story of Spice*s (British Museum Press, 2000) by Andrew Dalby.

Cute took as its starting point a piece of grafitti on the toilet wall in The Bull (now The Queen Boadicea), St John Street, London, EC1.

Tyrol is based on of the twenty-second section of *What the Moon Saw* by Hans Christian Andersen.

Tied-Up House is based on the song of the same name by Jackie Leven, which appears on his album *Shining Brother Shining Sister* (Cooking Vinyl, 2003).

Against Complaint is derived from the translation of a Yoruba poem ('Variety: why do we grumble') included in *The Penguin Book of Oral Poetry*, ed. R Finnegan (Penguin, 1978).

Jackpot was constructed from two previous unsuccessful poems (one of the same title and 'Ecstatic Sketch').

Shoreline Charismatic arose from a conversation (and notes thereon) with the poets Mererid Hopwood and Matthew Welton on a walk to the coast during a BFI Poetry and Film weekend at Ty Newydd.

Salt is a homeopathic version of the poem 'Love like Salt' by Lisel Mueller, from *Alive Together: New and Selected Poems* (LSU Press, 1996)

Hunter's Stew is a version of a short section of the 19th century epic *Pan Tadeusz* by Adam Mickiewicz, loosely based on a doggerel translation reproduced in *An Exaltation of Soups* (Three Rivers Press, 2004) by Patricia Solley.

Keepsakes started from a question on a quiz machine, "If you fly due west from Tierra del Fuego, what is the next piece of land you will reach?"

The Boon of the Wind was developed from its opening lines which came to me in a dream.

At the Heroes of Folklore Meet-up borrows its structure from the poem 'I Did Brain Surgery On A Barnsley Pub Floor' from the collection *Harmonica* (Wrecking Ball Press, 2003) by Geoff Hattersley.

Cavian was influenced by the song lyrics of Nick Cave.

Poem Beginning With a Line By Roddy Lumsden starts as announced, and then comprises lines (with some changes in punctuation) from poems by Catherine Wagner, Brenda Shaughnessy, Kate Lilley, Louise Glück, Martha Ronk, Emma Lew, Susan Wheeler, Vickie Karp and Sarah Manguso.

Coster Colony is derived from a passage in Henry Mayhew's *London Labour and the London Poor* (Penguin Classics).

To the Sea is an overlay, adapted from a statement on 'the nature of love' by 19th century orator Henry Ward Beecher.

Also available from Donut Press

Stranded in Sub-Atomica, by Tim Turnbull.
£10 (plus £1 P&P)

Boys' Night Out in the Afternoon, by Tim Wells.
£10 (plus £1 P&P)

The Observations of Aleksandr Svetlov, by Colette Bryce.
£5 (plus £1 P&P)

A Voids Officer Achieves the Tree Pose, by Annie Freud.
£5 (plus £1 P&P)

The Glutton's Daughter, by Sinéad Wilson.
£5 (plus £1 P&P)

What was that?, by Tim Turnbull.
£5 (plus £1 P&P)

Buffalo Bills, by John Stammers.
£5 (plus £1 P&P)

The Switch, by Jonathan Asser.
£4 (plus £1 P&P)

Cheques, POs and IMOs payable to Donut Press.
Donut Press, PO Box 45093, London, N4 1UZ.

Donut press

www.donutpress.co.uk